HUMAN DUALITY

Two Plays

By

T. Gordon Mayhall

Human Duality

A Starving Writers Book / Published by arrangement with the author

Cover design by Starving Writers Publishing

Starving Writers Publishing: Athens, Texas

www.starvingwriters.net

ISBN: 1-932996-04-4

Printed in the United States of America

Published in Athens, Texas

*About the Author *

T. Gordon Mayhall was born in Lawton, Oklahoma in 1982 and raised most of his life in Athens, Texas. He is the son of an East Texas Fishing guide and a Family Law Lawyer. He was educated at Lon Morris College and Trinity Valley College studying English, and Performing Arts. He has been a professional stage actor and director since high school and continues to act while pursuing a writing career

T. Gordon Mayhall's first published book was Renegade 2-6, published in the summer of 2004. It is a performing arts piece about finding the humanity in the apathy and madness of war. T. Gordon Mayhall is also a professional bartender while being a full time writer and actor. He makes his home on Athens Texas, but travels between Dallas Texas and New York City most of the year.

Renegade 2-6

Its 1969, during a time of madness, and 9 men must make the choice to fight or to run. Set in Vietnam during the war these men bicker amongst themselves on a daily basis, but find a way to work together only to find out that they are going to die. For duty, for friendship, they make the hardest choice of their lives, but they are always ready to send the last letter home.

Please keep in mind that the language in this story is raw and not very grammatical, symbolizing how the people in this time and place, and in this type of situation would really talk. The characters in this story are not very educated and use a perverse way to express themselves.

Conscious Thoughts

While faced with the choice of having to give up his dream of being a writer when his life takes a surprising and unexpected turn one man will play out the scenarios in his mind of the choices he can make. They are the conscious choices that will lead to his own demise or joyful success, for they are his own Conscious Thoughts. With everything that can go wrong for him or everything that can be right for him, for his family, and for his dream he will have to make the right choice in order to find success and to find his happiness.

Table of Contents

Forward to Renegade 2-6

The true Human experience is always seen through our conflicts whether it be war, or a person's inner turmoil, or even our own emotional destruction. We are defined by our actions within those kinds of experiences. Renegade 2-6 is a great example of the Human element taking place within a destructive time. Like Steinbeck and Hemmingway T. Gordon Mayhall shows us that ideals are still just as relevant among the realists. War may be hell, but the human soul still thrives as long as we let it even through the madness of our times. For an idealist like me it has been a great pleasure to be one of the first to take part in the Renegade 2-6 experience.

Marcus Blake

Renegade 2-6

By

T. Gordon Mayhall

A Play in Two Acts

Setting

It's in Vietnam in 1969 on a rocky hillside, in the heart of this war torn country.

The troops are guarding a bridge that leads to a South Vietnamese town; they're protecting it from VC inhabitants. The Play portrays life during the Vietnam War, through the eyes of a small unit stationed directly in the path of fighting. These men each come from different parts of the country and are finally brought together as one.

Characters

Chief

Sgt. Eric Williams is from Salt Lake City Utah, 23 years old and a Black Man. He is a strong willed man who is always following orders and he is the backbone of the group, who never strays from his job.

Padre

Pvt. Raymond Sanchez is from Chicago Illinois and is a 22 year old Hispanic Man. He is a Preacher from the Chicago area that Volunteered for service, he is the faithful one and eventually rubs off on all of them.

Zig Zag

PFC Shawn Cole Sr. is from Harlem New York and a 19 year old Black Man. He is the one among the group that smokes weed in tight spots and is not afraid to say what is on his mind...no matter how he feels.

Ace

Pvt. Bradley Thompson is from Houston Texas and is an 18 year old White Man. He is really scared in the beginning, but he eventually shows his bravery and is the sole survivor of the group.

Tex

Cpl. John Evan Smith is from Sister Dale, Texas and a 25 year old country White Man. He is surprisingly really smart, and he is scared of dying, but not afraid to lay his life on the line for his friends and fellow Soldiers. Dale, Texas and a 25 year old country White Man. He is surprisingly really smart, and he is scared of dying, but not afraid to lay his life on the line for his friends and fellow Soldiers.

Mother

Cpl. Ben Thomas is from Seattle Washington, and a 24 year old White Man. He is a man who is pretty simple, he is the voice in Chiefs ear, he and Eric are best friends, and they go back a long way.

Doc

Cpl. Kevin James is from Philadelphia Pennsylvania, and a 22 year old Black Man He is a real outspoken man, who believes in Civil Rights of all men; not just for black men but for all men.

Screw

Pvt. Juan Garcia is from San Diego California and a 20 year old Hispanic Man. He is real full of himself, but he is really optimistic.

Mox

Lt. .Abbott Moxy is from Tampa, Florida and a 29 year old White Man.

1st Man

One of the men that enters with Ace at the end.

Beth

Zig Zag's Wife, a Black Woman

U.S. Soldier One – extra soldier

U.S. Soldier Two - extra soldier

U.S. Soldier Three - extra soldier

U.S. Soldier Four- extra soldier

U.S. Soldier Five - extra soldier

VC One - extra soldier

VC Two - extra soldier

VC Three - extra soldier

VC Four- extra soldier

VC Five - extra soldier

Act 1

Scene 1

The lights are down and we hear gunfire and screaming, we hear Ace crying, while we hear Tex shouting out obscenities. As the lights come up we see a man lying face down in the dirt, its Mox. Mother, Zig Zag, Padre and Screw are still shooting while, Tex, Chief and Doc are all reloading their rifles getting ready to shoot again. Ace is behind a tree crying, Mox is lying right next to him. The shooting stops and we still hear Screw shooting.

Chief -Cease Fire, cease fire ***(Screw is the only one still shooting)*** Goddamn it would you stop shooting.

Screw- ***(to the VC)*** To hell with all of you, you bitch ass pricks. ***(He lets off a few more rounds.)***

Chief- Would you stop already ***(All gets quiet)*** Mox, Mox; Damnitt Mox.

Mother- ***(He peeks over his post to see Mox dead)*** Mox is down Chief...Over there ***(pointing to where Mox is lying dead)***

Screw- You mother *fuckers!* ***(He pulls off one of his grenades and chucks it stage left where we hear an explosion)*** You need "cajones" like this.
(He starts pointing at his crotch, as Chief grabs him.)

Chief- What are you, stupid, we're low on ammo as it is. Do you realize that the grenade you just wasted could have been the deciding factor of whether or not we live or die? ***(There is a brief pause)*** Think about it.

Chief walks over to Mox's corpse

Screw- Sorry Chief, damn ***(looking at Mox's dead body.)***

Chief- ***(Looks over at Mox)*** Shit! ***(Looks at Ace who is still sitting down whimpering a bit.)*** Get up son. You got many long nights ahead of you. Radio in, tell'em Mox is down and ask what are the options? If we are to maintain our post, request fresh bodies, but until the jury is done deliberating I am assuming command. Doc, you Zig Zag, and Padre give Mox a little processional. Tex and Mother, let's secure the area.

Ace -And me, Chief?

Chief- -Stay here and make sure Screw doesn't screw up the orders.

Tex-That's steak and potatoes you Mexican prick. ***(He laughs, they all exit.)***

Screw- ***(Yelling it out)*** I'm from Spain, you ass hole! ***(To Ace)*** Can you believe those guys sometimes.

Ace- I don't know, can I.

Screw- In battle yes, in life hell no. They have your back until your wife writes you a letter saying that she is leaving you for one of those hippy assholes.

Ace- I wouldn't know about that.

Screw- Oh that's right fish. You came fresh off of grandpa's farm huh. ***(To the radio)*** Renegade 2-6 to Eagle 8-5. ***(radio)*** Over, Papa bear is down, I repeat, Papa bear is down ***(radio)*** over, should we move the plantation north. ***(radio)*** Well in that case we need slaves to keep this plantation alive, the heat is killing all of our cotton. ***(Radio)*** Well shit, 2-6 out. ***(Puts radio down.)*** Shit!

Ace- What?

Screw- Oh Well, Chief's in charge, we are to hold our position until further notice and they can't spare bodies. So we're screwed in more ways than one

Ace-I knew I was going to die out here. I just knew it.

Screw-Don't worry about it Kid; one way or another, we're going down in the history books, like Washington and Jefferson except we're not going to die in battle (***He chuckles.***)

Ace-They didn't die in battle.

Screw-But they sure as hell died of old age!

Ace-What are you trying to say.

Screw-Hell I don't know, but after this war we're all going to be famous, for shutting down communism once again.

Ace-I don't know about that, I heard Mox and Chief talking last night...Mox said that we are probably going to lose this bridge, and if we lose this bridge, then we'll probably all die, and he said something about the war already being lost.

Screw- Ah, that's horse shit ***(Chief, Mother and Tex all enter.)*** How many of them sons of bitches did I hit.

Tex-You didn't take anything but I know I cleaned 5 chink's clocks.

Ace-They're Vietnamese.

Tex-Shut up titty baby ***(he starts making a crying sound)*** Wah, wah, I wanna go home so I can suck on mama's titty again.

Ace- My mom is dead you prick ***(He gets up to charge Tex and is held back by Mother.)***

Screw- Kick his ass fish.

Tex- You wanna go son, I'll show you how grandpa works that paddle.

Chief-Both of you stop it, and that's an order.

Ace- ***(Ace sits back down)*** Yes sergeant.

Tex-You know I don't take too kindly to niggers given orders.

Before the words can even leave his mouth, chief already has his hand on the back of Tex's head and a pistol to the bottom of his chin.

Chief- ***(Doc, Zig Zag and Padre enter.)*** Son, right now you don't have two good legs to stand on so I'd shut up if I were you. You ever hear of Webster you know writes dictionaries. ***(Tex nods yes)*** His definition of nigger goes something like this," someone who is ignorant and too stupid to speak." Do I seem that way to you? ***(Tex gives no response.)*** So help me if I hear you say that to either me or one of my colleagues…Well let's just say that I'm not afraid to shoot you and say that you were a casualty of war, are we clear?

Tex-Yes sergeant, my sincerest apologies!

Chief- ***(He gives a nod of approval to Tex)*** Screw, what's the status on this whole operation "screw" Renegade 2-6?

Screw-I'm glad you asked sir, because well frankly we better make room for one more dick, because they're screwing us even more. I have confirmation, you are in charge. 1st we have to hold our position, 2nd we can't have any relief because apparently we are now in between two VC camps.

Doc-Hold our position, what the hell is this...it's just like the US government to screw us over.

Zig Zag-You know what this calls for. ***(He pulls out a joint and lights it up)*** Just like I always say, if you're getting screwed, why not be stoned too

Padre-I think God will watch over us, we just have to pray.

Screw-Amen, you just gotta live life day by day, and if it is your day to go, or mine...well, I'm sure God will be more than happy to greet you at the pearly gates.

Padre-And if not heaven, I'm sure Satan would be more than happy to watch you burn for the rest of eternity

Everybody starts to laugh.

Mother-So we gotta secure a bridge, while getting our asses shot at from both sides.

Chief- Yeah and we are going to still take orders from the top and hold our position.

Doc- You know we're gonna be buried out here. And nobody is gonna even know. Before I left, Canada started sounding nicer and nicer with each passing day Damn it I knew I should have moved.

Chief-Well it's too late for that, so we might as well start taking orders.

Doc-I try to take orders, but when you are still being oppressed by a government and fighting for them they should at least give you the benefit of the doubt, and know that when you're screwed, you're screwed, and it's time to get out.

Tex- Calm down Malcolm. Why don't you quit being shoved and start pushing back.

Doc-What the hell are you trying to say?

Chief-He's saying, that you need to stop complaining to us, and stand up to the people that are making this shit possible.

Doc-I would, but I can't.

Zig Zag-What do you mean?

Doc-Are you all blind? Don't not know that all of us are going to die out here.

Screw-Someone is pessimistic.

Doc-Open your eyes, this dirt and mud we're standing on the last piece of earth we're going to see. And that donkey we saw last week is going to be the last piece of ass we see.

Zig Zag- So that's why she didn't take my number?

They all laugh

Doc-*(Seriously)* When are you going to see the light when you're lying face down in the dirt? What the hell is wrong with you people?

Doc is so mad that he goes to his post behind the sand bags

Ace-What's wrong with him?

Chief-Nothing fish ***(Chief walks over to Doc*)** Look, I can't help that we are stuck in this situation, but I'll try my damnedest to make sure that we all get out of this alive.

Chief turns to walk away but is stopped by Doc.

Doc- Don't make any promises you can't keep.

Chief-*(Chief pauses for a bit and continues on to the group)* All right enough dick'in around, if we want to get out of this alive, we are going to have to play it safe. Everybody man your post; Don't move for any reason unless you want to get shot by me personally. Ya dig.

All-Yes sergeant.

Chief-You eat when I say you eat, you piss when I say you piss. I'll give our guys thirty-six hours to provide us with the resources we need. After that we're moving out. Orders or no orders!

Mother- ***(To chief, who is right beside him)*** I'll be damned, did that boy finally talk some sense into you.

Chief-Shut up you prick.

Mother-No, I think you gotta crush all right and at least somebody's falling in love.

Chief-And somebody is about to get shot!

They both laugh

Tex-Somebody said something about last piece of ass earlier ***(reminiscing)*** Man, I remember my last piece, a little senorita from Luckenbach, she was as hot as fire, a prize no doubt, she could suck a golf ball through a garden hose, definitely my kinda pleasure.

Mother-I remember mine, it was a girl from Salt Lake City. She was a big voluptuous woman and she was as black as night; she could get busy until the early morning sun. This mistress of mine had a name that would give her pleasure, Aretha.

Chief- Hey that's my mother's name.

Everybody except chief laughs as he finally gets it.

Chief- You bitch! ***(He starts to laugh)***

Padre-I remember my last piece of ass!

Screw-What's that preacher man.

Padre-Oh yes, even the good minister needs some good loving from time to time. Pamela, now that girl was a charm. She came into my office one day and sat down and began talking with me about my sermon, the past Sunday...well eventually we got on the subject of her doing the church thing. Well before you knew it she was doing the church thing ***(referring to himself...they all laugh)*** We had many more discussions after that.

Zig Zag- So you been banging the sisters huh preacher man?

Ace-How is that!

Padre-Well they say to practice what you preach, and if you come to any of my sermons you'll know that I never preach on fornication.

They all laugh again.

Tex-What about you fish?

Ace- ***(Stunned)*** What! Oh, um, you see, um

Zig Zag- ***(as if saying it over a loud speaker, cupping his mouth)*** We have a virgin, I repeat, we have a virgin

They all laugh.

Ace-You guys can stop now...it's not exactly something I am particularly proud of.

Screw-Man that has got to suck...I remember my last piece of ass; it was my wife's cousin Lolita, now that was some prime rump roast there.

Doc-How can you cheat on your wife like that?

Screw-Easy! She cheated on me first with my best friend Carlos, so I say what goes around always comes around. Anyway, Carlos is a big, hippy now. ***(Quoting Carlos)*** Stop the hatred, stop the war ***(Laughing)*** Fuck that big prick.

Zig Zag-I'll bet he's got a big prick too, that's probably why your wife likes him better than you. ***(They all start to laugh)*** I remember my last time; it was probably the worst I ever got, my wife man. She just couldn't understand why I was leaving her. She just kept crying, saying that I didn't love her and asking why I didn't just get a divorce (He kind of goes off into his own little world) I did love her and I still do. And now I have a son, and I can't wait to get back to see her smiling face and his too. She was probably the best thing that could have ever happened to an idiot like me. Coming here could have been the single most idiotic thing I could have ever done.

Ace- ***(Really interested)*** Why did she think that you didn't love her?

Zig Zag-Don't worry about it.

Chief- ***(Pulling out a picture)*** Last girl I got with was Rachel Ann. I jerk off to her picture every night.

Mother - ***(Looking at the picture)*** Oh yeah, me too.
They all laugh.

Doc-Last woman I ever slept with was a beautiful young white woman.

Zig Zag - What.

Doc-Oh yeah, Susan, man she was hot ***(Whispering)*** She said I had the biggest dick she had ever seen. (Everybody is saying things like...no; nuh uh; that bitch is a lie, what, etc.) No shit man, the biggest.

Chief-I'm sure that can't stand next to my Utah rattlesnake.

Screw- ***(Stepping out of his post)*** Nothing like my brass balls

He laughs, and at that moment bullets start to fly and he is struck in the back of the head.

Chief-Shit! Medic, now!

Doc runs to Screw and pulls him back to his post and starts to work on him as the others return fire.

Doc-No use chief, head shot.

Tex-Die you spic hating mothers

He is saying this while he is shooting and crossing to another post

Chief-goddamn it, we don't need another dead hero. Stay at your post, unless ordered out.

He continues to return fire as more fire is being returned.

Mother-Chief, I sure do miss your mama.

Zig Zag-Got one.

Chief-Shut the hell up and keep shooting

Ace-Grenade!

A grenade lands in between them all, he picks it up and throws it back.

Ace-Have a nice day asshole.

He ducks back into his hole as the grenade goes off, the shooting stops.

Padre-Well dip me in honey and call me Shirley Rook, I think you just knocked off a whole VC unit.

Ace-*(Getting excited)* Really?

Padre-Naw, they probably just scattered, but you can think that if you want to.

Ace-Well, I think I will.

Chief-Ace and Doc, I want you to man your positions. Zig Zag, you and Tex take Screw out to graze, find his letter and give it to me. Mother, padre, you're with me...Understood!

All-Yes sergeant.

They all exit.

Ace-What do you think about all of this, honestly?

Doc-*(Pause)* I think its bull shit, what about you?

Ace-That thing that you said earlier, about us all being blind, I see what you are talking about. I know that if we stay her, we're all going to wind up like Screw and Mox, or Reagan and Pearl. It's just a matter of time.

Doc-You know before I came here, I was on my way to getting my doctorate in political science. I could have been something, I would no longer be known as a little black nigger boy. I would be known as Dr. Kevin James. You realize, I could be the missing link to Civil Rights. All of this black Panthers bull shit, of black power. That's horse shit, what we need is unity, but we can't get it while your people are still oppressing mine. What we need is someone to step up and run for governor, or congressman. Maybe one day, president, but we're a dying breed, who only needs an ounce of step-up juice and we'd flourish.

Ace-I've never heard a black man speak like you before.

Doc-That's because in southern states you try to keep your black men dumb. You know if we would just work together we might just find a black Albert Einstein or a Black Charles Lindbergh, black people are smart enough.

You know black people had to be pretty smart to come over here, and learn to read and write in a foreign language and speak it. The slave owners kept close eyes on the slaves to make sure they didn't learn anything except how to work, but they hid their knowledge, and eventually used it to escape. At that time it seemed like the only man who had the right idea was Abe Lincoln. When he abolished slavery, he wasn't trying to say for the black man to take over, he was merely saying for us to take our rightful place at the table. ***(Tex and Zig Zag enter)*** I'm not here to say that your four fathers were wrong for not abolishing slavery, but I am trying to say that it would have saved a lot of trouble and a lot of lives over a ridiculous war.

Zig Zag-Preach on brother, preach on.

Tex-Please don't.

Doc-As soon as we got out of slavery we tried to step up, but we kept getting held back by your people.

Tex-When are you going to learn that the stuff you're saying over here makes no difference, because the only people that hear you are people that are probably never going to have to worry about that again.

Doc-Prime example of a slave owner close-minded always has to be in control.

Tex-This is what I am talking about, you're placing the blame on me, for the fault of my ancestors What the hell do you expect me to do invent a time machine and go back in time so I can slap some sense into my ancestors, just to say. "What are you fucking stupid?" No, your people have been out of slavery for a little over a hundred years and you still haven't done anything. And you're about preaching unity, but when are you going to stop saying," your people" and "my people" and start saying "our people".

Doc - ***(Stunned)*** That was probably the greatest response I have ever heard. If we make it out of here alive do you mind if I use some of that.

Tex - Sure.

Zig Zag- ***(to Doc)*** I could have swore he was nothing more than a hillbilly.

Ace- I didn't even think he had a brain.

Tex- Screw you.

The lights go down

End of Act 1 Scene 1

Scene 2

During the blackout we hear gunfire, little spurts of gunfire

Chief- Clear.

Then we hear a few more shots

Padre- Clear.

Then we hear mother scream and fire a lot of rounds off.

Mother- Godamnitt, I'm clear.

The lights finally come back up; Tex, Doc, Ace and Zig Zag are still in the same spots. Zig Zag is rolling another joint. Tex is over by Doc and Ace is over by Zig Zag. Chief and Padre are holding up Mother, who is limping, as they enter.

Ace- Oh Shit, What happened?

Mother-That VC prick stabbed me in the foot before I could kill him Doc goes over to check mother out as chief and padre return to their posts.

Doc- Take off your shoe ***(Mother takes off the shoe on the good foot.)*** The other one dimwit. He takes off his other shoe then Doc cleans up the wound and wraps it in gauze

Padre- Well Ace, you didn't kill all of them, but you wounded a whole crap load of them.

Chief- Way to think on your toes son, if you would have balled up like you did last time, we might all be dead.

Ace-Thank You Chief.

Doc-You can put your shoes back on now; it's just a flesh wound. It should heal in a couple of days.

Mother puts his shoes back on.

Padre- I knew you were faking it.

Chief- Goes to show the next time you cry wolf we might not be there.

Mother- I didn't cry wolf! That bitch stabbed me. He would have stabbed me again had I not put a couple of holes in his head.

Tex- Alright, pussy boy.

Chief- So what the hell are you all doing standing out in the open, do we not take orders any more?

They all head back to their post.

Ace- ***(Looking around)*** Its starting to get dark.

Tex- Are you scared of the dark?

Ace- ***(Quickly)*** No, What's it to ya?

Tex- I was just asking cuz I didn't want to be the only one.

They all laugh

Chief- Zig Zag, you and I are gonna stand guard tonight. Come over here so Mother can go over there ***(To Mother)*** I'm sure you'd be able to elevate your foot a little better on that big ass rock over there than on this little one here. You don't have that long to sleep gents so rest your eyelids and be ready for anything. Mother is helped over to Zig Zag's post by ZigZag and then Zig Zag goes over to Chief's post.

Tex- Good night folks!

Ace- Night Tex night every body.

Chief- Would you quit saying good night and just fucking go to sleep.

Padre- ***(In a girls voice)*** Good night Chiefy poo.

They all laugh

Chief- ***(In a solemn Voice)*** Good night my little soldiers. ***(Now in a stern voice)*** Now go to sleep.

Immediately people are already asleep. You can tell by the sounds they make because they are not obnoxious or loud.

Chief- I'm sorry about keeping you up...It's just that I didn't think I would be able to stay up by myself.

Zig Zag- ***(He lights up a joint)*** it's all right chief. I haven't been sleeping very good lately anyway.

Chief- How's that?

Zig Zag- Well, I received a letter from my wife before we left for this location.

Chief- About what, is she leaving you?

Zig Zag- Well she's thinking about it? Not because she is cheating on me, but because, well she doesn't think that I love her. See before I left, we were going through some tough times and I didn't tell her I was coming over here, until a couple of days before I left, and without any explanation. So she thinks that I left because I didn't want to be with her, which isn't entirely true.

Chief- What do you man?

Zig Zag- Well, I love her, more than ever, but I'm not sure that we can work out or problems. We have a son, one that I haven't even met yet.

Chief- What's his name?

Zig Zag- Shawn Demetrius Cole, Jr. I have his picture. ***(He pulls a picture out of his shirt pocket and hands it to chief)*** That's my boy.

Chief- Who's that gorgeous woman?

Zig Zag-That's my wife Beth. We dated all through high school then we got married. We were having some real problems before I left because I was an alcoholic. She was so beautiful and whenever I got drunk, I would get jealous and be a real asshole to her.

Chief- Why don't you quit drinking?

Zig Zag- Oh I did, whenever I got over her, but then I found weed and that's a subtle anecdote...marijuana really calms me down, I really want to be with her, if nothing else for the sake of our son.

Chief- Well what seems to be the problem, I mean, I see it as you just serve your time and get out of here.

Zig Zag- It's not that simple, every since the first day I've been here, I've had this feeling that I wasn't going to make it out of here alive so I wrote this letter, ***(He pulls a letter out of his helmet)*** and I have been looking for someone who will deliver it personally, and that person, will be asked to watch over my son as his godfather.

Chief- you are totally jumping the gun; you only have a month left and you're headed back.

Zig Zag- I trust you a lot, so take this, ***(He put the letter in Chiefs hands)*** and please deliver it to my wife.

Chief- No you're gonna make it out of here.

Zig Zag- If I do make it out of here no worries I'd still like a visit from you after you get out anyway. If I don't I'll have some one that I can trust protect and watch over my family, but if you sleep with my wife I will kill you in your dreams.

Chief- ***(he laughs but is still hesitant then he finally agrees)*** All right!

Ace- ***(Whispering)*** Chief, can I take a piss, please!

Chief- All right, but stick close to your post. ***(To Zig Zag)*** I'll do it, but only on one condition. Whenever you do get back home, you reconcile with your wife. You've already found your solution, now go back and fix the problem.

While Ace is peeing, bullets wiz past his head, he immediately jumps back to his post.

Ace- Shit!!!

As the bullets start flying, they all wake up syncopated, and they return fire.

Chief- ***(He looks over and sees them the VC advancing on them)*** They're advancing, shit. Tex, gooks six o'clock.

Tex steps out of his post while still shooting and throws a grenade off Stage Left, and then hops back to his post.

Tex- *(yelling)* Here Chinky, chinky, chinky. ***(He looks over at Ace who is staring back at him with a grin)*** Don't even say it.

Without anyone seeing it, the grenade is tossed back on stage, behind the sand bags and Doc.

Mother- This is for all you pricks out there.

He shoots some more as the grenade explodes behind him, in Doc's post throwing doc into the air.

Tex- ***(Tex runs over to Doc and drags him back to his post while still shooting his own gun)*** Die you assholes ***(He steps out to shoot once more but the shooting stops)***

Chief- Cease-fire, cease-fire. ***(The gunfire completely stops)***

Doc- ***(In pain)*** Godamnit. I'm the medic; this isn't supposed to happen to me.

Tex- Hang in there buddy, you're gonna make it man.

Doc- ***(his voice is slowly getting worse with his health)*** No I'm not. Have you even looked at my back?

He starts spitting up blood and going into convulsions.

Tex- Don't say that, you're gonna make it. ***(Tex is becoming very teary eyed and almost crying)*** Come on man, who am I gonna call stupid if you leave, huh. Who am I gonna debate with you can't do this. ***(Doc closes his eyes and is dead.)*** Don't do this, ah shit.

He picks up Doc over his shoulder and carries him off stage right

Chief- Padre go with him.

Padre- yes sergeant

Ace- I'm going too, sergeant

Zig Zag- Me too sergeant

Chief- Alright!

They all exit.

Mother- Eric ***(He doesn't listen)*** godamnit Eric. ***(Chief turns to Mother)*** You know what we need to do?

Chief-Ben, I have orders.

Mother- We need to get the hell out of here and you know we do.

Chief- I have orders.

Mother- Screw your orders. It's time to go Eric.

Chief- No!

Mother- This is your best friend speaking, I wouldn't tell you this unless I absolutely meant it. We need to leave.

Chief- It's not that simple; it is nothing like when we were kids. We have people to answer to.

Mother- Kids, the last two guys we just lost were kids. Remember we got in this together as a fun thing to do. It's not fun anymore.

Chief- I'm ready to go just as much as you are, so don't even start.

Mother- Then let's go; you have that decision ma king power now fuck'in do it.

Chief- We're gonna carry out our orders and stay.

Mother- For how long, until we're all dead.

Chief- ***(Standing up)*** you shut up. You know I don't want that now just drop it.

End of Act 1 Scene 2

Scene 3

Mother and Chief are sitting in the Dark, we hear padre talking in the dark; sort of like it's a funeral.

Padre- and father, please guide his soul to better places, in your precious name dear Lord, Amen.

The lights come up as Padre, Tex, Zig Zag and Ace enter. They all come in and Take their post and all sit for about 30 seconds in pure silence, thinking about the men they just lost and if 'they' are going to live. Mother is very upset along with Tex and Zig Zag, Chief is very frustrated, Padre is feeling the moment and Ace is just confused.

Tex- So what's the verdict Chief, are we going to keep falling, are we going to keep dying? ***(Chief avoids the question)*** Hey, answer me. ***(Tex gets up from his post and gets in Chiefs face)*** What the hell are you doing, get up and get us outta here.

Padre goes and pulls Tex back

Padre- This isn't going to help. We can't start arguing amongst ourselves.

Tex- Then explain to me what the just happened back there, huh. He was obliterated by my grenade. How the hell is the US Army going to explain that one to his parents, He had the makings of a great leader and in one fatal swoop, it all disappeared. He knew how screwed up this mission was. He told you and me and everybody else here.

Zig Zag- Chief, he's speaking some sense

Chief- About what? ***(He stands up)*** About us getting out of here, about Doc dying or about explaining to his parents how it happened. I know. I fuck'in know. But I made a promise, a promise to my superiors, before God and every single one of you that I would perform my duties and do them to the best of my abilities under any circumstances. You Mother, you were definitely there. I am not going to be pushed around by these gooks or any of my men to prevent me from doing those duties. Not you ***(To Tex)*** or you ***(To Mother)*** or any body. Now I am going to take my orders and deal with them in the best manner I know how to whether you like it or not, and go about my business. By my watch any of you men are free to go, so by no means don't let me hold you back. But I guarantee that what is out there is far worse than anything I could do to you so you take your high horses and you ride into the sunset, just as quickly as you rode in. Do you understand?

Zig Zag- ***(Yelling)*** Then what are we gonna do, Are we gonna take orders until we all die or what!

Chief- ***(Calmly)*** I'll tell you what we're gonna do. 12 hours, that's all I ask of you. That's all I want. You stay with me 12 hours and if no relief has come, then we're outta here. We're not sticking around to see anybody; not Charlie or not any relief.

Ace- Aren't you going against our orders?

Chief- I'll Tell them how it's gonna be. Believe me they'll know. (***He goes and picks up the radio and brings it back to his post.)*** Renegade 2-6 to Eagle 8-5 ***(Radio)*** We're in a rut here, we need more men, and now.(Radio) No you listen to me we're gone in 12 hours, like it or not unless we get some god damn help out here. ***(Radio)*** You do that and throw away the key while you are at it. You can strap me to the chair and turn on the juice, but at least I would know that my men got out of here alive. ***(Radio)*** 12 hours, that's it, over and out. ***(He throws the radio across the stage every once in a while the radio goes off)*** Don't anybody answer that until we have confirmation from them about fresh bodies.

All- Yes sergeant!

Chief- 12 hours gentlemen, that's all I ask.

Mother- I'm with you.

Tex- Me too!

Zig Zag- me too!

Padre- May God be with us.

Ace- Amen.

Chief- Now if we are going to make it out of this alive, you're going to have to follow my orders, are we clear?

All- Yes sergeant

Chief- Every shot we make is going to have to count, because we are low on ammo. Don't make stupid choices men stay at your post. Ace, you're the new radioman and listen to what those bureaucratic assholes have to say. Zig Zag, I need you behind those bags back there; that's the safest place, you're the medic.

Zig Zag- But I don't know what to do. I've never done this before.

Chief- Smoke a joint and pray. Tex, I need you to be the eyes and voice of this body, if you see anything unusual, grenade, two sided attack anything, I need a name or location or what ever it is. Loudly son, you gotta speak over all the noise we need to hear it Padre.

Padre- Yes sergeant

Chief- You're my front man, get up there, ***(He points to the object closest to Stage Left)*** Take this. ***(He throws him a shotgun)*** You'll need it. I need you to shoot as many of them as you can. Mother, you're in charge of grenades. I tell you where to throw them and help Tex look for anything suspicious. God gives you free will and so do I. You better accept these orders.

All- Yes sergeant.

Chief- Very well, we're gonna make it outta here gentlemen.

There's a Long pause.

Ace- Padre, are you a preacher or a priest?

Padre- Preacher, why?

]

Ace- Well, it's just that, I never was a Christian and I never believed in God, but I think I want to.

Padre- Well, all you have to do is be baptized, confess your sins and repent from your old ways. Above all you must believe that Jesus is the Savior.

Tex- What does repent mean.

Padre- It means to sort of like, turn your back on your old ways.

Ace- Who was Jesus?

Padre- Well, Jesus was sort of like a modern day hippy, except he didn't smoke weed.

Zig Zag- Hey that was never proven.

Padre- And he didn't lobby against stupid things He fought against the persecution of men and for their sins.

Chief- So what is baptism and what is so special about that?

Padre- Well you know how Jesus died and rose again on the third day. ***(He gets a very vague response)*** Well, Jesus died on the cross, and just like him we are hanging there with all of our sins and debts, but when he died and was buried in his tomb. We also are like that, except we are buried in the water; when we come out of the water we are resurrected just as Jesus was, into a new life free of sin and debt.

Zig Zag- So I don't have to pay the IRS?

Padre- Not worldly debts but all of your spiritual debts, but you can't have one without the other three.

Mother- How do you get baptized?

Padre- Well, in the Bible, it says you must be completely immersed. ***(He holds up his canteen)*** But I'm pretty sure Jesus would make an exception if any of you would like to be saved I think I have enough here.

Ace- I think I would.

Chief- What could it hurt?

Zig Zag- I've already been baptized, but I would like to confess my sins.

Tex- I reckon, I've already been saved myself.

Mother- Could he heal me?

Padre- It might take a while, but yes, I'm sure he could.

Ace- Could he get us out of here alive?

Padre- *(looks at chief and answers)* No one knows the Lord's will for our lives; all we can do is pray and wish. Is every one sure?

All- Yes!

Padre- Alright, let's begin with prayer. Dear Lord, we come before you today to finally join in your glory, and bask in your love. We pray that you will guide us through these tough times and help us out in this situation we are in. If that be your will, guide us and teach us dear lord. It is in your holy precious name dear lord, Amen. ***(To Chief)*** Are you ready?

Chief- Yes!

Padre walks over to Chief and extends a hand in friendship at him.

Padre- Sgt. Eric Williams, I have one question for you, do you believe that Jesus is the Christ, the son of the living God and do you accept him as your lord and Savior?

Chief- I do!

Padre- Then I baptize you in the name of the Father, and of the Son and the Holy Spirit. ***(He pours a little water from his canteen over Chiefs head)*** Welcome to the family of God! Ace, are you ready?

Ace- Yes!

Padre- ***(He walks over to Ace)*** Pvt. Bradley Thompson, Do you believe that Jesus is the Christ, the son of the living God and do you accept him as your Lord and Savior.

Ace- I do!

Padre- Then I baptize you in the name of t***he father, and of the son and the Holy Spirit. (He pours a little water from his canteen over Ace's head)*** Welcome to the family of God! Mother, are you ready.

Mother, nods his head in approval, and as he stands up to await the arrival of Padre, he is shot in the stomach and falls down. the shooting continues.

Chief- Oh shit! ***(They all start shooting back)***

Tex- Stand down Padre!

Padre dives over into Ace's post with Ace. Tex runs over to Mothers post to help stop the bleeding, but on his way over he is shot in the left leg and in the left arm, and then he falls to the ground, He doesn't get shot again in this fight.

Chief- Zig Zag, grab him! ***(Referring to Tex)*** Ben, are you all right....***(Zig Zag grabs Tex, and brings him back to Tex's post,***

whenever he gets there, Mother lets out a blood curdling cry...and the shooting stops) Cease-fire, Cease-fire. ***(Chief runs to Mother's side and holds him up)*** Ben, Ben speak to me, please.

Mother- ***(He is dying)*** Padre, Padre please continue.***(Zig Zag runs over to him and tries to start working on him)*** No, I'm dying.

Padre- ***(He walks over to Mother and leans down to him)*** Cpl. Benjamin Thomas, Do you believe that Jesus is the Christ, the son of the living God and do you accept him as your Lord and Savior?

Mother- Yes!

Padre- Then I baptize you in the name of the Father, and of the Son and the Holy Spirit. ***(He pours a little water from his canteen over Mother's head)*** Welcome to the family of God!

Before he can even get the words out, Mother is dead.

Chief- Ben, Ben. ***(Yelling)*** Damnitt Ben, open your eyes Ben

Chief is hysterically crying now and rocking Mother back and forth as the men watch in anguish. Tex is the only one who isn't paying attention. He is talking to him self out loud.

Tex- ***(White spot on Tex)*** I'm wounded; do you know what it is like to be wounded? I wish they would have gone ahead and killed me. I'm gonna be crippled! I think they left me alive for a reason; to slow you all down. If we leave, they will catch up to us; if we stay, I'll be the first to go of all of us that are alive. I'll be the first to go. ***(He starts to cry)*** I don't want you all to die, so just go, leave me here and go. ***(The white spot turns to red)*** So go, get out of here. ***(Yelling)*** Leave godamnitt ***(Back to Normal)*** I'm not going to die by some VC prick. ***(Looking to God***) They're gonna have to do better than that. I only die by the hands of God or by my own and I don't see lightning, so all of you go. ***(He pulls out his pistol and looks at it for a few seconds)*** Dear God. ***(Crying even more)*** Please forgive me for all of my sins and for the one that I am about to commit. Please watch over these men and get them out of here safely if that be your will. Please Again; please forgive me for what I am about to do. ***(He sticks the gun to the bottom of his chin)*** Amen!

He pulls the trigger and dies right there. All the men react, some pick up their guns and other duck and some look straight at him as he shoots him self.

Chief- *(Screaming)* Why!

The scream lingers as the lights go out

End of Act 1 Scene 3

Act 2

Scene 1

As the lights come up we see Tex and Mother still on Stage and Padre is sitting at post praying. Chief is very solemn, Ace is sitting at his post listening to the radio, and Zig Zag is looking at pictures of his wife and child. There's another long pause to set the mood of the scene.

Zig Zag-They were right you know ***(He pulls out a joint and lights it up)*** You knew they were right. We should have left after they shot screw; hell, we should have left after Reagan and Pearl died. ***(Pause)*** They're playing Cat and Mouse with us.

Chief- Don't you think I know that, huh? Do you think, I am that stupid of a leader to not know that. I didn't get this rank by not knowing what cat and mouse was.

Zig Zag-All I'm Saying is.

Chief- ***(Yelling)*** godamnitt, I know what you are saying and you know what you're right we're leaving Zig Zag you grab Tex. I'll grab Mother. Padre and Ace.

Ace- Wait a sec Chief. I think I got something

He pulls off the headset and tosses the radio to Chief.

Chief- Renegade 2-6 to Eagle 8-5, go ahead

8-5. ***(Radio)*** In the vicinity. ***(To the men)*** I hope you all are ready to get out of here. (He throws the radio down to Ace) Kid, I hope you are ready for what I am about to tell you.

Ace- What?

Chief- You have to stay. Me, Padre and Zig Zag are all being re-stationed, but you are assuming command of the outfit that is coming. So in order to earn your stripes, you have to go and get them about a mile north of here their chopper will be there in roughly 20 minutes.

Ace- What?

Zig Zag- Why aren't we all going?

Chief- Because someone has to hold down the bridge until he gets back.

Padre- When do we leave?

Chief- When he gets back, our Chopper will be here at the same drop zone in 2 hours.

Zig Zag- Why didn't they send one of us, we are more experienced than the kid?

Ace- I can do it.

Zig Zag- Nobody is saying you can't; it is just that I don't want to stay here and I know none of you do. With Three people here we are liable to get ambushed. We don't know how many of them there are out there ***(Getting upset again)*** and I thought we were leaving anyway. What the hell happened to that?

Chief- We are, but this time we actually have a way out so kid you better take off right now.

Ace- Since I am in command, I agree with Zig Zag. Let's pack up and get the hell outta here.

Chief- First of all you are not in command yet, second of all, you have superiors to answer to. Thirdly you have to go find those other men so I would get a move on if I were you. ***(He writes something down, balls it up and throws it over to Ace)*** Read it and torch it!

Ace- What is it?

Chief- Coordinates dip shit!

Ace- Oh!

As soon as Ace lights the paper on fire, shooting starts. Everyone is shooting back, when he notices Ace is still standing there shooting.

Chief-What the hell are you doing, go!! ***(He has an idea)*** Wait., wait, wait; Zig Zag, act like you just got shot.

Zig Zag- What?

Chief- Just do it (Zig Zag stands up to act like he is getting shot...but instead of pretending, he really does get shot in the stomach) Nobody notices that he is really shot; the shooting stops and Chief thinks that his plan worked so he signals Ace to leave. Ace does so, exiting Stage Right. Zig Zag, stands up and crawls out of his post, and heads for chief who is looking Stage Left, Padre, turns to look Stage Right, just as Zig Zag hits, the floor.)

Padre- Oh Shit! ***(Chief turns around and sees Zig Zag).***
Chief- Man are we screwed ***(Runs over to Zig Zag and lifts his head up to Padre)*** Med-kit, now!

Padre- Yes sergeant ***(He runs to Zig Zag's post and grabs the med-kit, and then returns to Chiefs side)*** Here.

Chief- ***(To Zig Zag)*** We're gonna get you through this kid! ***(He stars working on him)***

Zig Zag- You know my kid will be a year old in November. That'll be 5 years I have known his mom. ***(Chief is still working very frantically.)*** Angela Beth Crawford Cole; God I love that woman. ***(To Chief)*** How could she not know that? I wished I could go back and change it all; I would if I could. I really hope you'll take care of my son. ***(Crying)*** I'm dying Chief; you broke you're promise so don't break another one. Please don't do that. ***(Slowly fading)***

Chief - Hang in there Zig Zag, we're gonna get you through this.

Zig Zag- ***(To Chief, pulling letters from his satchel and handing them to Chief.)*** Here are all the letters of the men you requested; you already have mine. ***(Sinking)*** Now do the right thing. ***(He dies)***

Padre - No, no, no, no. ***(Angry Prayer)*** God, why are you doing this, what trouble have we caused you? How can we follow the laws of men, when they are so screwed up? What are you doing to us? Why are we here? What is the meaning of this test? ***(He begins crying and sinks to his knees)*** Our Father which art in Heaven, Hallowed be thy name, thy Kingdom come thy will be done on Earth as it is in Heaven. ***(Chief slowly joins in)*** give us this day, our daily bread, and forgive us our debts as we forgive our debtors, and lead us not into temptation, but deliver us from evil. For thine is the Kingdom, and the Power and the Glory, Forever, Amen. ***(Chief stands up and grabs Padre on the shoulder***

and they both walk over to Chiefs post.) You know this could have been avoided, we could have already left, and been done with this war.

Chief- ***(Very slowly)*** I know!!

Padre- No you don't, couldn't you see the tell tale signs, the little bitty hints, for Christ's sake, your own men told you. They showed you the way and you turned your back on them. We're down to two men and you know we're going to die!! You know we are; I know we are. ***(He looks into Chiefs eyes and finally sees his weakness.)*** You know it to; you've known it all along, haven't you? **(Yelling)** Speak to me*!* ***(He gets no response; he grabs chief by the collar and slams him up against the rock, and sticks his knife to Chief's throat)*** I'm not afraid to slice your throat!!

Chief- ***(Beginning to cry)*** Alright, this isn't the first time this has happened to me. ***(Padre takes this like a dagger to the heart, he collapses)*** I met Mother in boot camp, and we just happened to be serving in the same unit! Alpha 5-1. We were protecting a little armory in Southern Vietnam, when we kept getting shot one by one, by one. We couldn't squeeze out for anything; we were down to one commanding officer, Mother and myself. It was at that time, ***(He's realizing)*** that I began taking the position my men are taking against me. VC made one more run killing our commander, and wounding Mother!!! So instead of sticking around, I rigged that armory up to explode, and Mother and I split. You know, I carried him for 2miles over my shoulder, through the heat and rain, running the entire way, to receive a field Accommodation for bravery and valor. I was promoted from private to sergeant in a little under 36 hours.

Padre- Why didn't you say anything, why not get us out of here! You've had 36 hours.

Chief- I was dumb then, we could've held that armory; we could have stopped them, all we had to do was hold out.

Padre- You did the right thing then, why can't you do the right thing now, what's holding you back?

Chief- orders!

Padre- You make the fucking orders, now make the right ones.

Chief- I can't!

Padre- Why not?

Chief- Because the first time they killed my commanding officer, and I had no orders I made'em up as I went and my top priority was to get my best friend out of harms way before I got in the way of death. I didn't want my friend to die!

Padre- ***(looking over at Mother)*** A lot of good you did him!

Chief- ***(Chief grabs Padre by the throat)*** Yeah and that was uncalled for!!

Padre Start's choking and Chief releases.

Padre- What!

Chief- Nothing!

Padre-What?

Chief- Just shut up for a while, give me time to think. ***(Padre turns to put his back against the wall and closes his eyes; he is already asleep.)*** What do I do!

Chief is quiet for a while, the lights slowly start to fade to a blue-wash. and then the gunfire starts up again. Padre and Chief wake up and start to return fire. Padre is hit in the leg he falls out into the open area and is shot several more times.

Chief- No!!!!! ***(The gunfire stops and Padre is dead)*** Shit! ***(Chief runs over to him and kneels down beside him.)*** Damnitt Padre! ***(To God)*** What are you doing to me, why are you doing this? I don't deserve this, I don't. ***(He stands up and begins weeping.)*** What do I do now!

This should be done as a recording, because they are voices he hears in his head. With each voice he sinks lower and lower until he is on both knees. The voices should be simultaneous, but it can be the director's decision

Zig Zag- *We should have left after they shot screw. Hell, we should have left after Reagan and Pearl died.*

Mother- *Screw your orders, it's time to go Eric.*

Tex- *He knew how screwed up this mission was. He told you and me and everybody else here*

Padre- *For Christ's sake, your own men told you...they showed you the way and you turned your back on them.*
Doc- *Are you going to wait to see the light until you're lying face down in the dirt.* ***(With Doc's last line Chief is on both knees.)***

Chief- *What do I do!*

All Simultaneously.

Zig Zag- *Go!*

Mother- *Get outta here!*

Tex- *Leave!*

Padre- *Don't stay here!*

Doc- *Get out now.*

Chief- ***(Still kneeling)*** Alright! ***(Yelling)*** Alright!

Chief starts to get up but as he does he is shot in the leg and put back down into the position and before he can grab his gun he is shot in the hea d.

Chief is dead. The men have died and we see Vietnamese start to come out from all directions. One of the VC goes straight to Chief and starts to search him, he finds the letters of the men; he starts to go through them. From Stage Right gunfire starts, they kill all the VC, the first to die is the one above Chief; after they are all down Ace and about 15 other men come from Stage Right; Ace walks over to Chief.

Ace- Men, don't get comfortable, we're not staying long. We're going after those assholes. ***(To the 1st man.)*** Grab that radio!!!

1st man- But those aren't our orders!

Ace- ***(Yelling at this kid)*** I make the fucking orders now, so we're moving out whether you want to or not!

All- Alright

Ace goes over to the VC that stole all the letters and takes the letters back.

Ace- You guys messed with the wrong country boy.

The lights go out

End of Act 2 Scene 1

Scene 2

One by one all of the men bring out letters to members of the audience and stand next to their chairs saluting as the letters are being read over the speaker system (pre-recorded.). Mox is the first one; to a lady.

Mox- Dear beloved wife of mine, if you are receiving this your husband is not coming home to you. I really want to see your beautiful face for one last time; I hate to tell you this, because, even in death, my love for you will hold on for the rest of eternity. I cry at nights, because I know that you are going to be receiving this letter anyway and it seems a lost cause. That is what this war is, nothing but miles of red tape and excuses. I will always love you and regret ever being sent away from the most beautiful woman in the world. Your Loving Husband. Lt. Abbott "Mox" Moxley III.

Screw is next to a beautiful young girl

Screw- Dear Lola, I apologize for not being able to return to you. This letter means that I am a casualty of war. I wished that I could make love to you one more time so I could laugh at that cheating bitch of a wife I have. Picturing you naked was the only thing that kept me sane over here. One day I hope to see you again. Your Love Spaniard Forever, Pvt. Juan Carlos "Screw" Garcia.

Doc, to a mom and dad

Doc- Dear Mom and Dad, I am writing you a letter to describe his last few days here on this earth for they are grim and dark, with no way of turning around. I am stuck in this living hell of bureaucracy, and pain. Forgive me for not being the perfect son, but I love you very much. Let my people know that we need to stop preaching separatism and start to preach unity. I love you both very much and I apologize for not being able to return to you. Love, Dr. Kevin "Doc" James.

Mother, to a businessman

Mother- Dear Lyle, this is your worker and front line analyst, If you are receiving this, I regret to inform you that I will not be working for you ever again because, to bluntly put it, I am dead and honestly, I have no family worth writing too. So I figured I would write my former boss and friend. Print this in your paper if you don't mind. The men of Renegade 2-6, are men that fight bravely, but I fear that we will not be leaving this bridge. Sgt. Eric Williams, helped us through many troubled times but my fear has come true. I will not be writing you any more letters from the front line. Sincerely, Cpl. Benjamin "Mother" Thomas.

Tex, to his father

Tex- Dear Dad, if you are receiving this, your son has gone on to a better place. If you ever have any grand babies, don't forget to tell them about their Uncle John. Give Little Tex and Mama a kiss for me. With all my love Cpl. John Evan "Tex" Smith

Padre, to his brother

Padre- Dear Chris, if you are receiving this, your brother and best friend has gone to see Jesus. I pray that you follow in my footsteps, and go through the world, baptizing people in the name of Jesus. I have faith in you; dodge the draft at all costs. God's Eternal Servant, Rev. Raymond "Padre" Sanchez. P.S. Move to Canada.

Chief, to his mother

Chief- Dear Mama, if you are getting this, I am not going to be back. I'm sorry, tell my brothers and sisters that I'm dead, but love them and I will always miss them. One day, I will see you again if God will forgive me for my sins. Love your Son and Brother, Sgt. Eric Williams Jr.

Zig Zag is last, delivered by Ace to Beth. On stage Zig Zag, is behind them both saluting.

Zig Zag- Dear Beth, out of all women, I couldn't have found a more perfect one. I left because I was unsure of the situation we were in. Now I am afraid of not returning to it. You are the love of my life, and if you are receiving this my life has come to an end. (Beth collapses and is caught by Ace) Unlike my love for you, I never should have runaway. Let the man delivering this letter take care of my son, our son, and you. He is my friend and your shoulder to cry on. Let him teach our son how to be a better man than his father. Love Always, Pvt. 1st Class, Shawn Demetrius Cole, Sr.

The lights go out : End of Act 2 Scene 2

~The End~

Forward to Conscious Thoughts

There are only a few times that a particular story can make you stand back and think about all the choices you've made in your life. Then make you wonder how they led you to this point and if you've made the right choices. Most of us can answer the latter very quickly, but can we remember all the choice that we have faced and know without doubt whether they made the right or wrong difference in our lives, probably not. Conscious Thoughts is one of those stories that makes us ponder all the choices in our head that we can make and inspire us to weigh carefully the right one as to not lead us down the road to our own destruction. Like a modern day Tennessee Williams T. Gordon Mayhall shows us that although we cannot escape the agony in life our own destruction and our demons that come out of the night are ruled by the choices we make and what our conscious thoughts lead us to do. It is a powerful and emotional story; being apart of the editing and performance process has been a great pleasure and we thank T. Gordon Mayhall for inspiring us to carefully look at the choices we make so our lives do not end being our own destruction.

Richard Anderson and Jason Almgreen

Conscious Thoughts

By

T. Gordon Mayhall

With

Lauren A. Hopper

A Play in One Act

Characters

Adam- The son of John and Lauren and the narrator of the story (he reads the prologue at the beginning and the end)

John – The Writer of the story. Husband to Lauren and father to Adam

Lauren –Adam's Mother and John's wife

Annie – John's Mistress

Dr. Cates – Child Psychologist and the Adam's Psychologist

The Judge : The Judge presiding over Psychologist Adam's custody case

O. A. –Opposing Attorney and Lauren's Attorney in Adam's custody case

Bailiff – The bailiff of the court in Adam's custody case

Doctor – The Doctor who delivers Adam when he's born

Prologue

Adam: Have you ever found yourself awakened in a dark room, lying on your back? You can't move, you can't hear and your heart isn't beating, but your thoughts continue. Your mind won't stop, it can't! Pre-birth and Post-death; is that all we have to look forward to? Is it such a struggle waking up next to the same woman everyday? Is it too hard to tell the truth? It seems as though a man finding himself in this day and age is almost impossible.

(A spotlight comes up SR on John typing on a typewriter, very fervently)

A woman taking the path most traveled is inevitable. The greatest lesson I have ever learned came from a man that had no time for his family, he never once showed me, but I taught him. You made your bed...now lie in it. ***(Pause)***

About fifteen years ago, in Small-town America, a young couple met for the first time. They grew together, as if it were meant to be. They had found each other, they couldn't wait any longer. They got married and the woman was very quickly with child ***(Chuckling.)***I'd say about two hours after the ceremony. He was a barkeep and writer; she was a receptionist for a local doctor. Their perfect world had finally come together. But the root of all evils would rear its ugly head and drive a wedge between the young lovers, forcing them to give up their dreams and at long last...each other. Without money, he had no choice but to sacrifice in order to preserve. He gave up his first love, writing, to make ends meet and he put himself through night school. On top of sacrificing his talent, he lost his family. It's not that they weren't there; he just didn't have time for them. After five years of night school and several jobs later, he became a lawyer. His dreams of writing had all but diminished, but the scars still remained. He found comfort in alcohol and eventually other women, one in particular. Is this you? ***(Pointing to the audience. The spot on John goes out.)***

You have your stories, and this is ours.

The lights go out, then a single spot rises Center Stage, with John in the middle and Lauren to his right facing in, and Annie to his left facing in.

John: I don't know where my heart lies,

Lauren: I don't know if you even care.

John: On one hand,

Annie: You have me.

John: on the other

Lauren: Your wife,

Annie: or your mistress...

John: The decision is up to me, but I can't choose.

Annie: Who do you love?

Lauren: Me? ***(Lauren freezes as John looks at her)***

John: I love...

Annie: or me! ***(Annie freezes as John looks at her)***

John: I love...I don't know, Sometimes I wonder if lust has just taken over...I lie awake at night staring at the ceiling thinking about the girl at the grocery store, or the woman who waits on us at the café...She has the most beautiful lips. But I never think about the woman lying next to me...she put herself outside of the picture I painted for my life. Why?

John freezes as Lauren unfreezes, her response is almost simultaneous.

Lauren: The man that I once revered, now hardly ever looks at me. The look that won me over, the look that saved me from a sea of drowning men...He used to have such a vision, a dream of success. Only to fail, only to fall...which is the reason why he is pushing himself away from me. I hear him at night, I know he isn't sleeping, I just wish I knew what he was thinking.

Lauren freezes as Annie unfreezes, Annie is pleading hers and John's case.

Annie: My husband is always gone, he never talks to me...so what was I to do? I found someone who would listen, someone who understood me. Did I mean to become romantically involved? Sometimes, I think yes. He seems so sensitive, so sweet. He gets me like my husband never could. The only problem is...

Lauren and John unfreeze; lines are very rapid one on top of the other.

John: What if my wife finds out?

Lauren: What are you hiding?

John: What if my son finds out?

Lauren: Why won't you talk to me?

John: Would she leave me after fifteen years of marriage?

Annie: I'm here for you....

John: What if her husband finds out?

Lauren: Say something...anything. ***(Lauren walks out of the spot light)***

John: I don't know.

Annie: what is it? ***(Annie walks out of the spot)***

John: I don't know. ***(John walks out of the spot)***

A bed rolls into the spot with Lauren lying in front of John facing the audience, Lauren looks asleep, while John is twiddling his thumbs, John leans up.

John: ***(Quietly)*** Psst...Lauren. ***(A little louder)*** Lauren...Are you asleep.

Lauren: I was.

John: I'm sorry, but I wanted to ask you something.

Lauren: It better not involve sex.

John: Would you listen, it's important!

Lauren: What?

John: Well, you know that I love you, and...

Lauren: yes!

John: ***(Stuttering)*** And well, I just wanted to know.

Lauren: Could you please speed this up, I have to get up in about five hours...

John: Would you let me finish...

Lauren: Talk away!

John: Alright as I was saying, you know I love you, ***(Stuttering again)*** and in the position that we're lying in...

Lauren: I told you no more sex...three times is plenty.

John: Damnit...would you let me finish?

Lauren: Alright.

John: ***(Stops stuttering)*** I just want you to marry me, will you marry me please?

Lauren: Okay. ***(She turns around to kiss him and then lies back down)***

John: That's it?

Lauren: I said yes, what do you want me to do?

John: Well a little more than what just happened.

Lauren: John, you know the one place I wish I was right now?

John: No, where?

Lauren: ***(She snuggles up next to him)*** I'm already here. I love you very much and nothing would make me happier than to walk down the aisle and stand next to you. I want to be with you for the rest of my life, and I will do whatever it takes to make this relationship work. ***(Playful)*** I love you more than any woman has ever loved a man; ***(She kisses him and lies back down in his arms)*** Was that better?

John: That was a bit better, thank you.

Lauren: Okay...good night. ***(John lies back down for a second)***

John: Lauren, **(He leans up again)**

Lauren: ***(Gentle)*** What?

John: Let's do it one more time.

Lauren: ***(Sharp)*** No!

John: You don't even have to think of it like sex...just think of it as a victory celebration.

Lauren: If that's the case, we've already had three victory celebrations, and my party favors are in need of a rest.

John: Okay. (He lies back down, pauses) Lauren.

Lauren: *(Angry)* Damnit John, what is it?

John: I love you.

Lauren: I love you, too.

The bed starts to roll off stage as John and Lauren stay in the spot light. They're held in place by ropes attached at the ankles. When they finally come off the bed they position themselves where they are back to back, with Lauren facing Stage Right and John facing Stage Left. Its now the Present time.

John: All this time I swore this relationship was one sided.

Lauren: I thought that our love would last forever!

John: How can she read me so well?

Lauren: Why doesn't he know?

John: I've done everything humanly possible.

Lauren: Except say that you love me.

The spot light fades out. Full stage lights come up to reveal their present Apartment, John is the only person on stage; he is sitting on the couch looking over the bills on the table, when Lauren walks in.

Lauren: Hey, how was your day?

John: Can't complain.

Lauren: Were we going to your parent's house this weekend?

John: No, I'm not going to be here this weekend...business trip.

Lauren: You've been leaving a lot here lately. Why do you feel the need to leave this house all the time?

John: Lauren, can we not do this now...I am struggling to keep this family afloat and with your constant nagging I can't do it.

Lauren: When are you going to?

John: Listen, I have to go to a client's house this weekend so I can get more information on the case.

Lauren: Why do you have to go this weekend, why can't you go another time, or have them come to your office?

John: We have to go to trial this coming Monday, and I have to know all the details on her case.

Lauren: On HER case, where are you staying?

John: I'm staying at HER house, is there a problem?

Lauren: Yes, there's a very big problem...

John: You're saying after fifteen years of marriage you still don't trust me?

Lauren: Why should I? You've become this secretive man ever since you started practicing law.

John: You're not supposed to share confidential information with anyone.

Lauren: I'm your wife!

John: Okay...but it's still confidential information.

Lauren: So, you're telling me that you can't give me a phone number where you're staying, or an address?

John: Why, so you can check on me every second?

Lauren: Why not, why can't I worry about my husband or wonder where he is?

(This is to be read as a scenario, not as truth while she is facing the audience) It's three o'clock in the morning, and you're just getting back from the office...but I've called up there several times and you still don't answer, I go up there and your car isn't there...Where are you? What are you hiding?

John: None of your damn business?

Lauren: Why not? Talk to me!

John: Talk to you about what?

Lauren: Haven't you been listening? I'm worried about where this relationship is headed. I'm worried about you, and above all, I'm worried about that boy in there. ***(She points to Adam's room)*** When is it going to end?

John: It may never end, ***(He starts to walk out the door)*** but this dream that you wanted costs money...I thought maybe we could make it on love, but it didn't work, it was never meant to work...so we'll just leave it at that.

Lauren: I've told you several times, this isn't what I want, I just want you.

John: You don't want a house to sleep in or food in your refrigerator.

Lauren: Yes...yes, I do want that, but you want more. I'm satisfied with what we have...our house is almost paid for. We have, what, two more years left; we have nothing to worry about.

John: Well maybe I'll just quit the firm and take up writing again...

Lauren: Great, that's what I want. I want you here, with me and Adam.

John: You're being absurd, I was kidding. You know I can't write anymore.

Lauren: Why not? You're a great writer, why can't you continue with it?

John: *(Sharp comeback)* Because I failed. I was no good.

Lauren: You didn't fail; you just didn't have time with a child and wife to support. But now I can work. The doctor's office pays me more than enough to support you and Adam.

John: ***(He starts to laugh)*** You support the family. ***(Laughs even more)*** That's a good one.

Lauren: ***(Snaps back)*** Are you saying my income wouldn't be good enough for you?

John: ***(He picks up the bills he was looking at)*** Not with these bills, or this mortgage, definitely not with this car note.

Lauren: ***(She starts to sob)*** I just want you here.

John: Well...now is not the time! ***(He walks out the front door, and slams the door behind him)***

Lauren: ***(She follows him out and has the door slammed in her face. She continues the argument by herself.)***

Why not now, this is the best time, this is the best place. Wake up you son of a bitch. This is reality calling, help me...help me please. I can't do this alone. I need you here with me. Now listen, listen to me please.

Adam walks in from his room to see his mother crying

Adam: ***(he creeps up beside her)*** Mom...mom, are you alright?

Lauren: ***(this startles her, she tries to pull herself back together, and she stands)*** Yes…yes

Adam: ***(sympathetic)*** Mom, tell me what's wrong?

Lauren: Your father ***(She swallows hard),*** I'm worried about your father.

Adam: What about him?

Lauren: I'm not sure your father will be... *(she starts to cry again and can't finish)*

Adam: What about him? *(She's still crying, Adam grabs her and holds her tightly)* It's going to be okay, mama. Everything's going to be okay.

Lauren: You're such a sweet boy.

The Lights fade out on the scene, A spot rises on John who is sitting at a typewriter writing, when Lauren comes up behind him and hugs him from behind and starts to tickle his ear John starts to laugh hysterically, then he turns around and forces her to the ground, playfully, and then he kisses her, she kisses him. Fifteen years earlier.

Lauren: I love you.

John: I love you too.

Lauren: What are you working on?

John: I'm writing a play.

Lauren: I know that, but what is it?

John: I don't know yet...I just thought of something and I started writing.

Lauren: Can I read it?

John: Not yet, but I promise you can read it when I'm done.

Lauren: You better.

John: ***(Playfully)*** Or what?

Lauren: Or you're just not getting any.

John: ***(He gasps)*** How could you?

Lauren: I'm just kidding. ***(She starts to laugh, and then waits for a bit)*** I'm pregnant.

John: ***(Bursts into laughter)*** Oh my God, you joke around way too much.

Lauren: ***(stops laughing)*** I wasn't joking.

John: ***(still trying to laugh, but not able to comprehend)*** So, you're telling me I'm going to be a dad? ***(She nods her head)*** I just...I didn't...how did this happen?

Lauren: Sex, John! ***(John still looks confused)*** Well, one night we were lying in bed...Need I say more?

John: Lauren...I know how it happened...I'm just dumbfounded.

Lauren: *(She closes her hands as if praying)* Dear Lord, please don't let my child be dumbfounded like his father.

John: You got all kinds of jokes don't you?

Lauren: Uh huh.

John: You're lucky I love you.

Lauren: You're lucky I put up with you.

John: ooh...I think I found a good scene to use...Do you want to read a little bit of this...

Lauren: Sure! ***(She reads a little bit)*** So I take it by first glance that the exclamation point and the dot, dot, dot are your fa vorite punctuation?

John: Yeah.

Lauren: Screw the period and comma, right? ***(John just stares at her with a loving gaze)*** What, do I have something on my face?

John: I just love you.

Lauren: Well, even though your head is abnormally large, I guess I feel the same about you....

John: ***(They smile at each other)*** You got all kinds of jokes don't you?

Lauren: I just hope they don't get old.

John: ***(Looking at his watch)*** Oh crap, I gotta go...job interview!

He kisses her again as he runs out of the spot, Lauren freezes. On the other side of the stage another spot comes up on Annie sitting at a table with two coffees in front of her, then John comes into the picture and sits down, he leans over the table and kisses her. Its the present time.

Annie: What are you doing? What if someone sees us?

John: I don't care...

Annie: What's the problem? You sounded pretty urgent on the phone.

John: Oh, my wife's just nagging me to death...something about, I'm never home...

Annie: Don't let it bother you. ***(Pause)***

John: ***(Stone faced)*** I think our marriage is over; I don't think I love her anymore.

Annie: Are you sure?

John: Yes I'm sure, she is constantly yelling at me...and well she won't… ***(Cuts him off)***

Annie: Maybe you just need to spend more time with her?

John: This is coming from the woman who is screwing her husband.

Annie: ***(Starting to get angry.)*** Is that all I am to you?

John: Well let's see, you're not my wife, so I guess you're just an easy lay.

Annie: You came to me...

John: Only after you sat in front of me waving your ass, and hitting on me.

Annie: You are such an asshole!

John: You know what, I'm tired of this, and I don't need this from you. I'm ending it with my wife, whether you or anyone approves. It's going to happen!

He gets up and walks out on her leaving her stunned. Both spot's go out, but come right back up. The typewriter is gone from Lauren's spot and she is the present day Lauren, while Annie is still somewhat sympathetic.

Annie: *(sympathetic)* I love you very much...

Lauren: *(Upset)* Why are you pushing yourself away from this family?

Annie: Let's just run away...come on?

Lauren: Stop running away from your problems.

Annie: You're my only escape.

Lauren: Why do you want to leave all the time?

Annie: Let's leave!

Lauren: Stop running!

Annie: Let's leave!

Lauren: Stop running!

The spots fade out as the lights come up on the apartment, Lauren is sitting alone on the couch in a house coat looking at her watch, really pissed off, and reading a magazine. John walks in.

Lauren: Where have you been?

John: Around...

Lauren: What made you come back?

John: Sadly enough, it was you...

Lauren: Why is that sad?

John: Lauren, I wanted to leave you tonight, but then I started thinking...my name is on the mortgage, not yours...so I'm going to ask you to leave my house.

Lauren: What?

John: ***(Very stern)*** I want a divorce. Please leave my house.

Lauren: I can't believe this. ***(She gets up and starts to walk to the room)***

John: Just leave my house and you can pick up your things tomorrow.

Lauren: You son of a bitch, why are you doing this?

John: It's over; our marriage has been dwindling for the past five years.

Lauren: Only because you let it happen.

John: That is such bullshit.

Lauren: You are the one who is pushing yourself away.

John: ***(Yelling)*** Exactly, now leave.

Lauren: How could you do this? I've been nothing but loyal to you, I've done nothing but whatever you ask.

John: Not everything.

Lauren: What do you mean?

John: I mean that you're never there for me.

Lauren: You're exactly right...because you're never around for me to be there for you. When did you intend on slowing down? When did YOU want a family? ***(Sensing the harsh reality of his response)*** Do you even want a family? If you didn't you shouldn't have knocked me up fifteen years ago.

The lights go out. We can hear Lauren screaming in the delivery room. A spot comes up to reveal Lauren in a delivery room, with John running in putting on his medical stuff, and a doctor sitting in front of Lauren. 15 years earlier.

John: See baby, I told you I wouldn't be late.

Lauren: ***(Starting to become painful)*** So what were you doing?

John: I was pushing my book idea to a publisher, who I met on the bus.

Lauren: ***(Breathing heavy)*** You really need a cell phone..

John: But those things are huge, where am I going to put it? ***(She starts to go into labor, screaming)*** Besides, I don't need to carry around a phone...You know, I'll always call you...have you seen the...

Lauren: Shut the hell up!

John: I can't believe…

Lauren: ***(Yelling)*** John! ***(Breathing heavy)*** You're not helping...

Doctor: Alright Mrs. Thomas, why don't you just push for me?

John: Come on, Baby.

Doctor: Push. ***(she screams and pushes all at the same time)***

Lauren: ***(She pushes again and starts to cry. She grabs the back of John's hair and starts to yank his head around.)*** Hold my hand! ***(Still yanking him around)***

John: I'm trying...but my head...

Doctor: Push!

John: No! ***(She grabs tightly onto his hair and yanks him down to the ground while she pushes...when she releases, she lets John back up and then slaps him with her free hand while yelling)***

Lauren: Why did you do this to me?

Doctor: You're almost there...let's push one more time...Ready?

John: Baby, can you let go of the hair?

Lauren: ***(Almost sounding evil)*** You stay out of this!

Doctor: Push!

She pushes again yanking John to the ground.

John: ***(Yelling)*** Aah! ***(She releases and lets John up still holding onto his hair, he tries to pull her hands off, Yelling back)*** Baby, please?

Lauren: *(Yelling)* You did this!

Doctor: Okay, Lauren, just one more good push and you can rest. Okay? Ready?

John: Doc, do I have to look forward to this next time?

Lauren: *(Sharp comeback, still breathing heavy)* No next time.

Doctor: Push...

She yanks John to the ground, for one final time, as they both yell, the lights go out. We hear a baby cry. The lights come back up on the present day apartment there is a knock at the door, John walks out of his room in night clothes or pajamas, he opens the door, and it is Annie.

John: What are you doing here?

Annie: Is she home?

John: Why, are you going to try and counsel us back together?

Annie: John, come on.

John: She left about an hour ago.

Annie: Good! ***(She drops her coat revealing a sexy nightgown, or outfit.)***

John: What are you doing? My son is In the other room.

Annie: ***(She snuggles up to him)*** Ah, come on.

John: What if Lauren..***(She cuts him off)***

Annie: Lauren who? In a couple of weeks, she's not going to matter.

John: Why are you doing this?

Annie: I felt bad for the way I acted today, I just wanted to make it up to you. ***(Adam walks out of his room, but no one sees him.)*** Please baby?

John: Alright, but no staying the night.

Annie: Okay baby.

She jumps into his arms and starts kissing him, Adam clears his throat to get their attention, John drops Annie.

John: Oh shit! ***(Adam storms back into his room slamming his door)*** ADAM! ***(Walking to the door)*** Adam, come on buddy. ***(Adam doesn't respond)*** Adam?

Annie: ***(Walking up behind John)*** Can I help?

John: No, in fact, you need to go. If I want custody of him, this cannot happen again until after the divorce is finalized.

Annie: When did you become Mr. Morals?

John: I'm an attorney, I know what it takes to win cases...and judges aren't sympathetic to men who cheat on their wives. So vamanos.

She picks up her trench coat and walks out...the lights go down except a spot on John, he walks to the cabinets and grabs a bottle of whiskey, he sits on the couch with a shot glass, between each line he takes a shot of whiskey.

John: ***(takes a shot)*** Oh my God what am I doing...how am I going to beat this? ***(Takes a shot)*** What am I going to do now, If he tells her about this, she'll surely get custody of him. ***(Takes a shot)*** I can't let that happen. ***(Takes a shot)*** Why did I do this to Lauren? She loves me, and I turned my back on her. ***(Takes a shot)*** Screw her! She doesn't deserve to be loved. ***(Takes a shot)*** She made me give it all up, she made me stop writing. ***(Takes a shot)*** It's her fault I hate myself!

The spot fades on John as another spot comes up on Lauren sleeping on a delivery room table, John walks in with an infant Adam in his arms, 15 years earlier.

John: Look buddy, its momma. That's your mama. She's so beautiful isn't she? You know, one of these days me and your mama are going to make it out of this dead old town, and eventually you won't have to worry about a thing...we're going to take good care of you. I love you...and I don't even know you...is that normal? Oh well.

The spot fades out as the scene ends

The lights come back up to reveal a present day courtroom where a custody hearing for Adam is taking place between John and Lauren

Judge: Mr. Thomas, it's your witness.

John: I would like to call Dr. Cates to the stand.

Dr. Cates walks from backstage and stands before the bailiff, he places his right hand on the Bible.

Bailiff: Do you solemnly swear, or affirm that the testimony you are about to give in this cause shall be the truth, the whole truth, and nothing but the truth so help you God?

Cates: I do.

Judge: You may be seated.

Cates: Thank you your honor.

The judge acknowledges with a nod.

John: Dr. Cates, would you state your full name for the record of the court?

Cates: Dr. William R. Cates.

John: And what is your profession?

Cates: I have a degree in child psychology.

John: Have you ever seen the child in question here?

Cates: Yes sir.

John: Have you had a chance to evaluate him and render your professional opinion?

Cates: Yes sir.

John: Can I get a brief summary of that evaluation?

Cates: In this case, it's hard to determine his emotional stability.

John: How many visits were you allowed with him?

Cates: I was allowed three visits, and within those visits I noticed certain traits related to social anxiety and extreme emotional instability.

John: How did you come to this conclusion?

Cates: Well, I can't give specifics, but I can tell you the little bits of information I am allotted to tell.

John: And those are?

Cates: He had a hard time controlling his mood, he has a lot of pent up anger, and he also holds a lot of sadness in his heart. His moods would often range from one side of the spectrum clear to the other side. He is a delicate teenager who has a lot of issues.

John: How would you go about controlling this?

Cates: I don't know!

Judge: "I don't know" is not a plausible answer in my court room.

Cates: I don't. You can't evaluate, treat, and cure someone in three visits.

John: How many visits then?

Cates: Judging from what I've already seen,... I'd say it could range from six months.... to three years.

John: Why such a wide range?

Cates: Well, honestly it took a while for him to even warm up to me and tell me certain facts about his life, and God only knows what he's not telling me. It could take months or even years to get him to open up to me and be completely honest. Only then could I reach a full analysis and determine a solution to this problem.

John: But still, why so long?

Cates: In my field, its trial and error, we could try 10 - 20 different medications before we see any results.

John: And how much do you think this medical expedition will cost?

Cates: At $300.00 a visit, and two visits per week we are looking at approximately $600.00 a week.

John: $600.00 a week?

Cates: Yes sir.*(He glances at Lauren and back at Cates.)* And that's not including medication.

John: Thank you Dr. Cates.... pass your honor.

(John sits down at his table and starts writing notes.)

Opposing Attorney: Thank you your honor. Dr. Cates, I would like to start with a few questions.

A spot light goes down on Lauren and John, one at each side of the stage as the lights go out. Lauren and John start arguing.

Lauren: How could you forget to call if you knew you were going to be late?

John: Why do I always have to call you? Why can't you call me?

Lauren: I do.. I did! Your secretary said you weren't there so I called again and she said you were in a meeting.

John: Well, I guess I was in a meeting.

Lauren: Its twelve o'clock at night John, and you told Adam you would go to his basketball game that ended over 3 ½ hours ago.

John: What do you expect me to do? Not go to the mediation, loose my client, my job, my license... Is that what you want??

The lights come back up to reveal the apartment.

Lauren: I want you home.

John: I'm home now.

Lauren: And your son is asleep...how many nights in the past week, no the past month have you been home to see your son?

John: I'm home every Sunday.

Lauren: Sunday! One day out of seven, and you don't even know what's going on with your son. Did you know that I was called up to the school today because he was fighting?

John: Did you punish him?

Lauren: Yes, he's grounded right now.

John: Why didn't you bust his butt?

Lauren: For Christ sake John, he's fifteen. Don't you think he's a little old?

John: No! ***(Yelling)*** Adam, get in here, NOW!

Adam: (Off stage, irritated) Coming!

Lauren: John, don't do this. I've already punished him.

John: Well, I don't think you did a good enough job.

Lauren: You weren't even here, how would you know?

Adam walks in groggy like he has been asleep.

Adam: Yes sir?

John: What happen at school today, why did you get into a fight?

Adam: I'm sorry.

John: Answer me!

Adam: I just... there was this dude, talking bad to this girl.

John: Was she your girlfriend?

Adam: No sir.

John: Was he hitting her?

Adam: No sir.

John: Who threw the first punch?

Adam: ***(Disappointed in himself)*** I did.

John: What did I tell you about starting fights?

Adam: Well.

John taps him on the forehead with his knuckle.

John: I told you, we don't start fights, we finish them.

Adam: I had to stand for her, no one else would.

John: Oh really?

Adam: Everybody else was just laughing at her.

Lauren: John, stop it please.

John: Don't do this in front of him, there is a chain of command here and he needs to understand that.

Lauren: John. ***(they start to go to their court room chairs again)***

John: Adam go to your room. If I hear about you fighting one more time I'll bust your ass so hard you won't be able to sit down for a week.

Adam walks to his room, the spot lights on the court room chairs come up as the lights go down.

John: Don't you dare try that again. When I'm punishing him you go along with it whether you like it or not.

Lauren: Don't cross examine our son and then pass judgment on him. This isn't a court room. He's your son, a boy that you're teaching to be a man.

John: ***(Yelling)*** I'm teaching him how to be a man.

Lauren: You're teaching him to be a rude, arrogant asshole.

John: I'm teaching him what I know and what I've learned.

Lauren: Is this what you learned from your father?

John: Yes!

Lauren: Well, I guess you learned all the wrong things then.

John: Objection your honor.

The lights come back up on the courtroom

John: That's irrelevant to the child's well being.

Judge: Over ruled.

O.A.: In that case, I have no further questions.

Judge: Mr. Thomas?

John: I'm done, your honor.

Judge: You may step down Mr. Cates.

Cates: Thank you your honor.

Judge: It's your witness Mr. Thomas

John: Your honor, I would like to call Mrs. Lauren Thomas.

Lauren can't believe she is being called up to the stand. She walks up and puts her right hand up and her left hand on the Bible.

Bailiff: Do you solemnly swear, or affirm that the testimony you are about to give in this cause shall be the truth, the whole truth, and nothing but the truth so help you God?

Lauren: I do.

Judge: You may be seated. Carry on Mr. Thomas.

John: Would you state your full name for the record of the court?

Lauren: Lauren Ashley Bremer Thomas

John: What is your profession?

Lauren: I am a receptionist for Lakeland Medical.

John: How many shifts do you work per week?

O.A.: Objection your honor, where is this going?

John: These are relevant questions your honor.

Judge: Sustained, hurry up and get to the point. Answer the question Mrs. Thomas.

Lauren: I work approximately four 8 hour shifts a week.

John: And how much is your average paycheck a week?

Lauren: Oh my God.

John: Your honor could you please instruct the witness to answer the question?

Judge: Mrs. Thomas?

Lauren: $450.00 a week after taxes.

O.A.: What is the relevance?

Judge: Were you listening to Dr. Cates testimony?

O.A.: Yes your honor!

John: ***(To Lauren)*** Did you hear the price quoted by Dr. Cates?

Lauren: I can't believe you are doing this.

John: Judge?

Lauren: Our son doesn't need psychological help.

Judge: Mrs. Thomas.

Lauren: He needs a father.

Judge: Mrs. Thomas, answer the question.

Lauren: Yes, yes I did.

John: Thank you. Do you have a current residence?

Lauren: Yes, I do. I live with my father.

John: How many bedrooms does this house have?

Lauren: How is this substantial? ***(Getting irate toward her attorney)*** Are you not going to say anything?

O.A.: ***(Standing)*** Objection.

Judge: Sustained.

O.A.: ***(Sitting)*** Okay.

Judge: I'm not going to tell you again Mrs. Thomas, one more outburst and you'll find yourself in a jail cell waiting to hear the outcome.

Lauren: One!

John: One, a single bedroom for three people. How do you propose to sleep?

Lauren: John...please, ***(Trying everything to keep from crying)*** you can have everything....just don't take my son.

John: Were you aware that your son had emotional problems?

Lauren: The only emotional… ***(He cuts her off)***

John: Judge?

Judge: I'm not going to tell you again Mrs. Thomas, simple question, simple answer.

Lauren: *(Yelling)* No.

John: If you weren't aware of the problem to begin with, how will you be prepared to deal with future problems?

Lauren: You're missing the point. I would do anything for my baby, and there was a time when I thought you felt the same way.

A spot rises on Lauren as the lights fade out.

Lauren: How could you have changed so dramatically? Why would you do something that you knew would affect us all? I would never ask you to stop doing what you love, especially if it means taking you away from the people you love.

A spot rises on John, 15 years earlier, typing on a type writer.

Lauren: I'm sorry I confused you with the man of my dreams...a great father and husband...You were, what happened?

We hear a baby stirring in John's spot light, Lauren starts to get really emotional.

Lauren: I used to love watching my two men learning to grow with each other.

John: Ssh.. I'm almost done buddy. ***(Continues typing)***

Lauren: I loved waking up at two...three o'clock in the morning, seeing you hold Adam. Telling him everything's okay, and then singing him to sleep. ***(Reminiscing)*** You may not know it, but I think you have a beautiful singing voice.

Lauren tries to push a smile through her tears.... Adam starts crying as Lauren's spot light goes out. John stops typing and walks out of his spot light then comes back with an infant Adam in his arms.

John: Ssh... Hey buddy, how was your sleep....huh? I'll bet your hungry aren't you baby? ***(He reaches beside the type writer and pulls out a bottle, Lauren walks in, with her house coat on. She doesn't say a word)*** What's this Adam? It looks like your baba...you want some?

He puts the bottle to his lips and Adam starts drinking. John starts to hum a tune. Lauren watches for a bit, then walks up behind him and puts her arms around him, and they start to dance....very small movement, but enough to tell. They look at each other and kiss. The lights fade out as they continue to dance.

We hear the gavel strike as the lights fade back up into the courtroom.

Judge: When a judge has to make this type of decision, it can often take a lot of sleepless nights. When the child's decision isn't in his best interest, a judge has to make a difficult choice. I can only tell you that my decision comes down to my best interest for the child. On one hand, we have the love of the mother and we all know that this mother's love is pure and genuine....but, as far as love goes...Can it pay the bills? Can one mother's love pay for the help that this child needs? Sure Mrs. Thomas, you can get two or three jobs to pay for the help, but won't that jeopardize the love and affection he has come to know and expect from his mother? In his darkest hours that love could quite possibly save his life and that is one that I can not completely abolish. Judging by the testimony given by Dr. Cates, we have no idea what's going on in this young troubled teen's mind. It could take a matter of years before he finally gets settled down. We don't know this. But on the opposite end of the spectrum, we have a father who is willing to spend and sacrifice whatever it takes to save this child from himself. And as I said earlier, I have to pass judgment not on the child's idea of his best interest, but my idea of the child's best interest. I think the child's best interest, is with his father. ***(Lauren breaks down into tears)*** I'm not terminating your parental rights. I wouldn't be able to sleep at night, if I didn't give you visitation rights, weekend custody, one month during the summer and two weeks during Christmas. Mrs. Thomas, what I have seen today is an excellent mother with true love for her son. Mr. Thomas, you will be expected to turn over your child to Mrs. Thomas every Friday at six o'clock p.m. and shall pick him up at 6:00 P.M.

every Sunday, at the mother's choice of pick up and delivery... we will work out the rest on paper and send you a copy.

John: Yes, your honor. ***(A spot comes up on John as the lights fade down, to Cates)*** Does he have a problem?

Dr. Cates walk into the spot as John pulls an envelope out of his jacket pocket full of money... Dr. Cates opens up the envelope and flips through the money.

Dr. Cates: Why yes, my expertise says he's going to need a lot of medical help.

John: How did you come to that conclusion?

Dr. Cates: I don't know, I'd have to meet him.

John smiles and Cates laughs. The spot goes out as a spot comes up on Lauren and Adam.

Adam: Let's go mom, let's just go, we'll leave the country, he'll never find us .

Lauren: But…

Adam: No buts mom!

Lauren: Well where would we go?

Adam: I don't know... France!

John walks into the picture

John: I've been there they hate Americans... it wouldn't work. Let's go!

Adam: Let me say goodbye.

John: Goodbye, c'mon! ***(He grabs Adam by the arm and carries him out of the spot)***

Lauren: I love you.

The spot fades out

The spot fades out as the lights go to a red out, and then we see John knocking on Adams door

John: Adam, get up...come on, it's time to get up. ***(The lights come up)*** You can't hide in there forever, you gotta go to school! Come on boy, your breakfast is getting cold!

Adam walks out of his room, with jeans on and a T-shirt in his hand.

Adam: You cooked breakfast, huh? ***(Sarcastic)*** Let me guess, this is the start of a whole new life for us isn't it?

John: Don't take that tone with me.

Adam: I thought that was the same tone you used with that Bimbo you screw every night. ***(John Slaps Adam)***

John: Don't say that, don't you dare say that.

Adam sits there stunned a bit, then he runs to his room and slams the door

Adam: Screw your breakfast!

John: Fine, fine...stay in there, I don't want to see your ass anyway.

He throws a huge tantrum, knocking over things and throwing stuff. He makes his way to the front of the stage, then the lights fade into a spot on John, for about 5 seconds where he is just breathing heavy from being so angry. Then the doorbell rings, the lights come back up on the house, John goes to answer the door, it's Lauren.

Lauren: Hey!

John: Can I help you?

Lauren: Can I come in?

John: Adam, get up...come on, it's time to get up. ***(The lights come up)*** You can't hide in there forever, you gotta go to school! Come on boy, your breakfast is getting cold!

Adam walks out of his room, with jeans on and a T-shirt in his hand.

Adam: You cooked breakfast, huh? ***(Sarcastic)*** Let me guess, this is the start of a whole new life for us isn't it?

John: Don't take that tone with me.

Adam: I thought that was the same tone you used with that Bimbo you screw every night. ***(John Slaps Adam)***

John: Don't say that, don't you dare say that.

Adam sits there stunned a bit, then he runs to his room and slams the door

Adam: Screw your breakfast!

John: Fine, fine...stay in there, I don't want to see your ass anyway.

He throws a huge tantrum, knocking over things and throwing stuff. He makes his way to the front of the stage, then the lights fade into a spot on John, for about 5 seconds where he is just breathing heavy from being so angry. Then the doorbell rings, the lights come back up on the house, John goes to answer the door, it's Lauren.

Lauren: Hey!

John: Can I help you?

Lauren: Can I come in?

Adam: Get out of my way. ***(Adam charges at his father, but is pushed down several times...then we hear a knock at the door. Adam stops)*** I hate you. ***(While John is distracted with answering the door Adam sneaks away to the other room where he shuts the door. John opens the door...it is Lauren again.)***

Lauren: Is everything okay?

John: Yes. ***(He shuts the door again, we hear Lauren knocking at the door)*** He's not here, go away. ***(The knocking stops)*** Adam...Adam, what are you doing in my room? ***(He goes to the door)*** Adam, open up...now!

The door flings open, and John jumps back a little bit, then we see Adam come out with a gun.

Adam: Sit down!

John: Now Adam, calm down!

Adam: Sit your ass down! ***(John sits down on the couch)*** Answer me this! Was it before or after you started screwing that slut, when you realized you didn't love my mother, your wife...to have and to hold until death do you part...does that mean anything to you?

John: Son, just calm down, please...we can talk about this...

Adam: Obviously, we can't.

We can hear Lauren knocking at the door

John: Maybe your mother can help ***(he gets up to go to the door)***

Adam: I told you to sit down. ***(He waves the gun in John's face)***

John: Okay, okay Adam. ***(he sits back down)***

Adam: You know, this isn't the first time I've thought about doing this.

John: Doing what, Adam?

Adam: You make my life a living hell, and you made my mothers a living hell. What do you have to say to that? What do you say to a son that only wants his father to acknowledge his existence?

John: Adam, I never meant to hurt you.

Adam: Well, you did. You let everybody down...including yourself. I only hope that you learn from this. I want you to know, that I do forgive you.

He puts the gun up to his head, and pulls the trigger as the lights go out and a spot comes up on John holding onto Adam's lifeless body

John: No, no, no, no, no...Why, why would you do this...why?

Then a spot comes up on Lauren who is holding an infant in her arms, she starts to sing her baby to sleep with the words below, When she is done with the words she begins to hum the tune then John joins her, as they both rock their babies to sleep.

John and Lauren: Close your eyes and go to sleep...Dream a dream a harmless dream. When you wake, I'll be here. To make your dreams come true.

They both finish the song just humming the words, as the spot slowly fades on Lauren, then the lights come back up on the judge's court bench, with just the bailiff and the judge presiding, John is still on the ground holding Adam.

Judge: ***(Very Harsh)*** For murder in the first, I sentence you to death. In the same manner that took the life of your victim, so shall that be your end. This is your demise!

The judge and the bailiff come over to John and throw him on the ground then the bailiff picks up the gun and hands it to the judge then the Judge puts the gun to his head. Adam gets up and walks over to the table where his father is and takes the place of the judge holding the gun to his head. The judge and bailiff start to walk backwards until out of the light.

Another spot comes up on the other side of the stage where Lauren is walking around with an infant Adam in her arms. John watches this scene while Adam speaks to him.

Adam: Do you know what it feels like to have a cold piece of steel pressed to your head, for hours, not knowing if you're going to pull the trigger or not. Not knowing if the person in the next room is going to even care. You put yourself in this situation. Now, can you get out of this!

The spot on Lauren goes out, while Adam walks out of his spot. By the end of the monologue John is alone, the light goes out the spot Lauren was in comes up with John holding an infant Adam rocking him to sleep, fifteen years earlier.

John: ***(To the baby)*** ssh...be quiet...ssh...it's okay ***(He starts humming a bit)*** ssh. ***(Lauren walks into the picture)***

Lauren: I knew you'd make a good father...

John: ***(He sets a quiet Adam down in the crib)*** How are we going to make this work? I mean where is all the money gonna come from?

Lauren: It's okay, we can do this...I know we can make it.

John: What are we gonna do for money?

Lauren: Well, You can walk the streets and I'll be your pimp. ***(They laugh a bit, she gets serious)*** Even if we have to work everyday for the rest of our lives, we'll be doing it together. We can do this, I believe it.

The scene blacks out, and opens back into the present living room where John is holding onto a dead Adam. Lauren is still outside and has become frantic.

Lauren: Let me in! ***(She jiggles the door knob and slams her palms against the door.)*** Let me in...what's going on? ***(Her voice leaves the front of the house...about 20 seconds later she emerges from the back of the house...And then we see her reaction to her husband holding her son's lifeless body. With***

a calm voice) Oh my God, my baby. What have you done? *(Yelling)* You killed my son!

John: ***(Scared, backs away from Adam, laying his head peacefully against the floor.)*** I...he...I don't...

Lauren: ***(She grabs her son and yells)*** Why are you sitting...call 9-1-1!

John picks up the phone and dials the number. We hear the other line over the speakers these next lines are so rapid.

911: 9-1-1, what's your emergency.

John: My son...

Lauren: (Yelling) You killed him...

John: My son shot himself...I need an ambulance.

Lauren: You did this...you did this, you son of a bitch!

John: Please I need an ambulance right now...

911: Sir, just calm down, were you a witness to the incident...

John: I don't have time to answer your questions, just get an ambulance over here now.

Lauren: Oh God, oh my God, why?

John slams the phone down, then he stops and tries to pick her up, she slaps him and starts to beat him up, he can do anything but just let it happen then the cops knock on the door, they hear the commotion and kick the door in, they take her off of him, they pick her up and John gets up and grabs a hold of Lauren. Once the cops take Lauren off of John, they can't stop staring at the body.

John: Please calm down...I didn't do it.

Lauren: You bastard! ***(She pushes herself out of his arms and walks out the door.)***

The lights fade out, end of scene, and then a scene change happens that turns the stage into a funeral home where Adam is in the casket, a spot comes up to show Lauren standing behind it. A hand is placed on her shoulder, as the lights come up, it is John.

John: ***(Very soothing)*** I'm here.

Lauren: ***(Getting upset)*** When? When were you here?

John: I'm here now.

Lauren: Not good enough. ***(Pause)*** I know about her...I know why you were gone all the time. Why did you do this? Was it me?

John: No...I don't.

Lauren: You don't know what to say do you?

John: Lauren, I can admit when I'm wrong...I was wrong in what I did and how I went about it.

Lauren: Well, it doesn't matter now, it's over.

John: Lauren, please...just give me one more chance.

Lauren: I hope you plan on leaving this world with nothing.

John: I love you.

Lauren: I loved you, too...but you spent your life pushing me away and hating yourself for it...

John: I'm sorry.

Lauren: That would've been nice to hear, had it been fifteen years ago...but your word is of no use to me now...I'm sorry that it had to end this way. I love you, but the smartest thing I can do is move on with my life.

John: How could we have not known about this when we met...How could we have overlooked our fate?

Lauren: We can't go back, it's over.

John: Could you ever forgive me?

Lauren: Why should I?

John: ***(Motioning to the casket, with Adam in it.)*** Because he already has.

Lauren: ***(Pause)*** I don't think you're ready for the guilt to end.

John: Please?

Lauren: Forgive yourself first.

Lauren walks out the door and as she is leaving she walks past Annie, Lauren stops looks at her and then leaves, John sits in a pew and doesn't notice the transfer that just happened, John starts to cry. Annie walks in behind John and puts her hand on his shoulder. John turns around to see her.

John: What are you doing here?

Annie: (Sympathetic) I just saw what happened...

John: (Getting Angry) What are you doing here?

Annie: I was worried about you. ***(She puts her arms around him)*** I know how you feel.

He slaps her hand away, and then moves down stage of her.

John: No you don't. How could you possibly know what it feels like to lose a child?

Annie: I don't.

John: And on top of that, being held responsible for his decision.

Annie: I don't, but I want to help you, I'll leave my husband...all you have to do is ask.

John: I don't want you to do that, I just want you to leave me alone. I want to quit playing this game.

Annie: You mean you don't want me anymore.

John: Annie you're being childish.

Annie: I love you.

John: No you don't, you love the idea of me...why, I'll never know. But you need to let it go. I'm done with this.

Annie: I'm not.

John: Annie you are going to wind up just like me if you continue on the path you are on.

Annie: I want to be with you, not away from you.

John: Annie, it's over.

Annie: Why?

John: ***(He cuts her off, yelling)*** Because you messed up my life.

Annie: I came to you because my husband never had time for me. I want someone like you who is always willing to listen.

John: ***(Still yelling)*** You turned me against the woman I promised to love forever. ***(Stops and becomes harsh without raising his voice)*** You turned me into your husband.

Annie shudders away from this as she walks off stage. Another spot comes up on Lauren, with the same spot on John. The lights dim to 40 %, continued from the beginning.

John: I never knew you loved me....

Lauren: Why should I even care,

John: My son died.

Lauren: He was my son too, you son of a bitch...You took him away from me.

John: I love you...please forgive me.

Lauren: Why should I?

John: ***(He looks at the coffin)*** Because I've learned to forgive myself.

The spots fade as the lights come Down to 20%, except for a spot Center Stage. Annie, Bailiff, Judge, O.A., the Doctor and Dr. Cates come on stage. We see Adam rise from the coffin, as all the players on stage strike a match and light a candle, we see Adam walk into the spot light. Once he is in the spotlight the lights go out revealing only the candles.

Adam: Did I want them to get back together...hopefully. Did I want them to find themselves...it would be nice. Did I want them to learn a life long lesson...now that would be intriguing.

A spot comes up on John, who has a typewriter in front of him. He starts to type the words Adam is saying. In Adams monologue it is the present, on John's typewriter it is fifteen years earlier.

Adam: You're sitting there and wondering what would make a boy of fifteen go crazy and kill himself...you wonder why I chose this path...simple. Because suicide was the only logical thing I could comprehend at the time. I very well might have saved my fathers life. I didn't do it for that...I did it, because I didn't think he loved me. In death, I am proven wrong.

Now John starts to speak with Adam, little by little we hear a baby crying.

John & Adam: He showed me the wrong way to do things but in the end showed himself the right way to live life. He found what was wrong, and made the change...that is the cause of his life...Could this be the end of a movie? Why is he talking of such things...Love, Hate, what could possibly end the insanity.

Adam slowly backs out of the spotlight leaving just John. Adam's spot goes out and the people with candles move offstage. John stops typing and starts reading the script.

John: I don't know what the end of this story could be, should my parents get back together, I would be grateful. ***(Finally, the baby gets so annoying that John can't help it.)*** Lauren, could I please have a little silence. ***(He goes back to reading)*** I really hope. Lauren, please...I'm almost done, please? ***(Silence)*** I really hope my life will be a lesson for some. ***(The lights come up on the apartment, Lauren walks in.)***

Lauren: ***(Whispered yelling)*** What is your problem, why couldn't you help me?

John: ***(Getting angry and talking loud)*** Well I'm almost done with… ***(Lauren cuts him off)***

Lauren: Baby...

John: *(Whispering)* I'm almost done with this, this is very important to me.

Lauren: More important than your family?

John: Yes ***(He thinks about this, and as if struck, he has an epiphany)*** No, no it's not. I'm sorry.

Lauren: It's okay.

John: Hey, I'm trying to figure out how to end this...would you like to help?

Lauren: Sure. ***(she looks at the script for a bit, and begins to read.)*** Do you think its okay to use your real name as the main character?

John: I don't know, I was thinking about changing it to Gordon.

Lauren: That sounds kinda flamboyant. ***(They start to laugh)***

A spot comes up on Lauren and John as the lights go out.

John: Just promise me you won't ask me to quit writing.

Lauren: I promise.

They hug and kiss, the lights fade as a spot light rises on Lauren and John as they just stand in their spots frozen, Adam walks into the spot and delivers the monologue.

Adam: My father looked back at his life and realized that he had only been scared of one thing...failure. He figured that if he ever went for his dreams, he would fail...it's in human nature. From the moment we're born, until the very instant we die, we're bound to fail. That's why God gives us free will, so we don't have to...The End.

Adam freezes in between his parents forming a family photo as the lights go out.

~The End~

Printed in the United States
212461BV00001B/151/A

9 781932 996043